NORWAY

FINLAND

SWEDEN

DENMARK

RLANDS

RUSSIAN

EMPIRE

Berlin ○

ologne

GERMAN EMPIRE

Warsaw ○

POLAND

CRLAND

AUSTRO – HUNGARIAN

EMPIRE

ITALY

Sarajevo ○

ROMANIA

SERBIA

MONTE-
NEGRO

BULGARIA

PERSIA

ALBANIA

OTTOMAN

GREECE

EMPIRE

Armistice

Written by Ruth Starke

Illustrated by David Kennett

working title press
An imprint of HarperCollins*Children'sBooks*

May 1954
Paris

In this book many voices tell the story of how the Great War of 1914–18 ended: let mine be the first. Why? Because as Chief Allied Interpreter at the signing of both the Armistice and the Treaty of Versailles I was a witness to history and in a unique position to record it, both formally, as interpreter, and in my own diary. But first, some necessary background.

The Great War started with what was referred to by some at the time as a 'Balkan Quarrel'. On 28 June 1914 the heir to the Austro-Hungarian throne, Archduke Franz Ferdinand, and his wife were in Sarajevo on a state visit to Bosnia when they were assassinated by a Serbian nationalist. It was a bad day for the royal family and a bad day for Europe, since it set in motion a slide towards war which eventually came to involve all the great powers. The war was fought in the Dardanelles and the Middle East between the British and Ottoman empires, and on the Western Front in France and Belgium between the Allies and the Germans. On the Eastern Front, Germany fought Austria-Hungary on one hand and Russia on the other. Colonial forces on both sides fought each other in East Africa. A prolonged German U-boat campaign in the Atlantic ultimately drew the United States of America into the war.

The war dragged on for four years, and after all the fighting the world was changed. Over 15,500 square kilometres of France were ruined; hundreds of villages were annihilated; large parts of East Africa were devastated. Governments toppled and empires fell. A revolution in Russia saw the downfall of Tsar Nicholas II and the rise of the Bolsheviks. Seventeen million were dead; millions more were maimed, traumatised, orphaned or widowed. Hospitals were crowded with wounded soldiers. One in every five Australians who fought was killed. Their bodies lay, or were buried, on battlefields far from home.

To the war-weary soldiers in their trenches, it seemed that the fighting would go on forever, but throughout October 1918 Allied troops advanced quickly through the last German line of retreat. The German forces finally collapsed, and with a revolution at home imminent, Germany's political leaders called for an armistice.

Paul Mantoux, Chief Allied Interpreter

Friday, 8 November 1918
Compiègne

The forest of Compiègne is approximately 60 kilometres north of Paris, not far from the front line but a world away from it. For this meeting the French have assembled a special train with a saloon car that was once the personal coach of Napoleon III; it is parked in a railway siding in the middle of the forest. The six envoys from Berlin have come to this secret location to face the Allied delegation.

Ferdinand Foch, Marshal of France and the Supreme Allied Commander, gives a salute and a curt bow to his enemies and asks them what they want. The Germans reply that they have come to discuss the terms of an armistice. But there will be no discussion. The thirty-four clauses of the Armistice have already been drawn up.

Marshal Foch is in a bad mood because his proposed terms to limit the power of Germany so that it would never again pose a threat to France have been rejected by the British and the Americans as too severe. Even so, the terms are crushing, and when they are read out to the Germans I can see by their faces that they are in shock.

Germany is given seventy-two hours to respond. Meanwhile, the fighting continues. How many more lives will be lost as we wait?

Paul Mantoux, Chief Allied Interpreter

Autumn 1918
West Flanders, Belgium

There are not many of the old hands left. I am the last of seven fellows from our class. Everyone talks of peace and armistice. All wait. If it again proves an illusion, then they will break up; hope is high, it cannot be taken away without an upheaval. If there is not peace, then there will be revolution.

Paul Bäumer, in Erich Maria Remarque's *All Quiet on the Western Front* (1929)

Autumn 1918
Berlin

We all long for peace but Opa says we Germans are like a man at the top of a steeple whose ladder has fallen away, and who cannot get down despite all his suffering. Mama says if the blockade doesn't end soon we will all die of starvation and fall off the steeple! All we eat, day after day, are boiled swedes. Ugh! Sometimes potatoes – the ration is one pound a week, and often they are rotten – and horrible bread we have to queue for. No meat at all.

Today an old horse fell down dead in the street and before you could blink people came streaming out of doorways armed with knives and cleavers and stripped the carcass clean. We heard that even the beloved kangaroos in the Berlin Zoo have been slaughtered for meat, poor creatures.

Nobody looks in a mirror any more. We are all of us just skin and bone, as pale and yellow as corpses.

Hedy Klein, 14

Monday, 11 November 1918 – 5.30 am
Compiègne

The Germans have signed! Yesterday they were shown newspapers from Paris with news of the Kaiser's abdication, and shortly afterwards they received instructions to sign from the new government in Berlin. Most of them have tears in their eyes but Marshal Foch, whose only son was killed in the first summer of the war, is unmoved, and he refuses to shake the hand of Matthias Erzberger, the head of the German delegation. 'Très bien,' he says. He waves his hand in dismissal. 'Eh bien, messieurs, c'est fini, allez.' Nobody needs me to translate, 'Very well, gentlemen, it's over, go.'

When they leave there is relief in the saloon car and, yes, excitement. We would, I think, toast the occasion if it were not so early in the morning!

A message is immediately transmitted to all Allied units by radio and telephone: 'Hostilities will stop on the entire front line beginning at 11 am, Paris time, November 11th.'

After 1,564 days and the loss of millions of lives, the Great War is over. I can only imagine the reaction all along the Western Front and at home!

Paul Mantoux, Chief Allied Interpreter

The Armistice at the Front

We fired the last barrages at 10.45 towards a small village called Hermeville. When the firing stopped all along the front lines it seemed so quiet it made me feel as if I'd suddenly been deprived of my ability to hear. The men looked at each other, and then a great cheer arose all along the line. Behind our position the French were dancing, shouting and waving bottles of wine.

Captain Harry S. Truman, Commander,
Battery D, 129th Field Artillery

My watch said nine o'clock. With only two hours to go, I drove over to the bank of the Meuse River to see the finish. The shelling was heavy and, as I walked down the road, it grew steadily worse. It seemed to me that every battery in the world was trying to burn up its guns. At last eleven o'clock came – but the firing continued. The men on both sides had decided to give each other all they had – their farewell to arms. It was a very natural impulse after their years of war, but unfortunately many fell after eleven o'clock that day.

Colonel Thomas Gowenlock,
Intelligence Officer,
American First Army Division

The troops received the announcement in *dead silence*, and almost with incredulity. It seemed impossible that the war should be over at last. ... From the quiet way in which the announcement was received it might have been thought that the troops were sorry that the war was ended. The truth of the matter was that the boys had become so used to the fact of war that they could hardly realise that the thing that they had so earnestly longed for had really happened.

Captain Walter C. Belford,
11th Battalion,
Australian Imperial Force

We had come through, we were still alive, and nobody at all would be killed tomorrow. ...We danced in the streets, embraced old women and pretty girls, swore blood brotherhood with soldiers in little bars, drank with our elbows locked in theirs, reeled through the streets with bottles of champagne ...

Malcolm Cowley, ambulance driver,
American Field Service

When 11 o'clock came, all was silent; not a gun to be heard, or any other sign of war. It seemed almost uncanny. The war – that long and bloody and ghastly war – was over! Not only over, but it had been won – decisively won – by us and our Allies! The Germans were defeated and crushed! The boastful, bragging Hun who had started and brought this bloody war on the world, was beaten and in the dust! How entirely comforting! How satisfactory!

Lieutenant Edward Allfree,
111th Siege Battery,
Royal Garrison Artillery

12

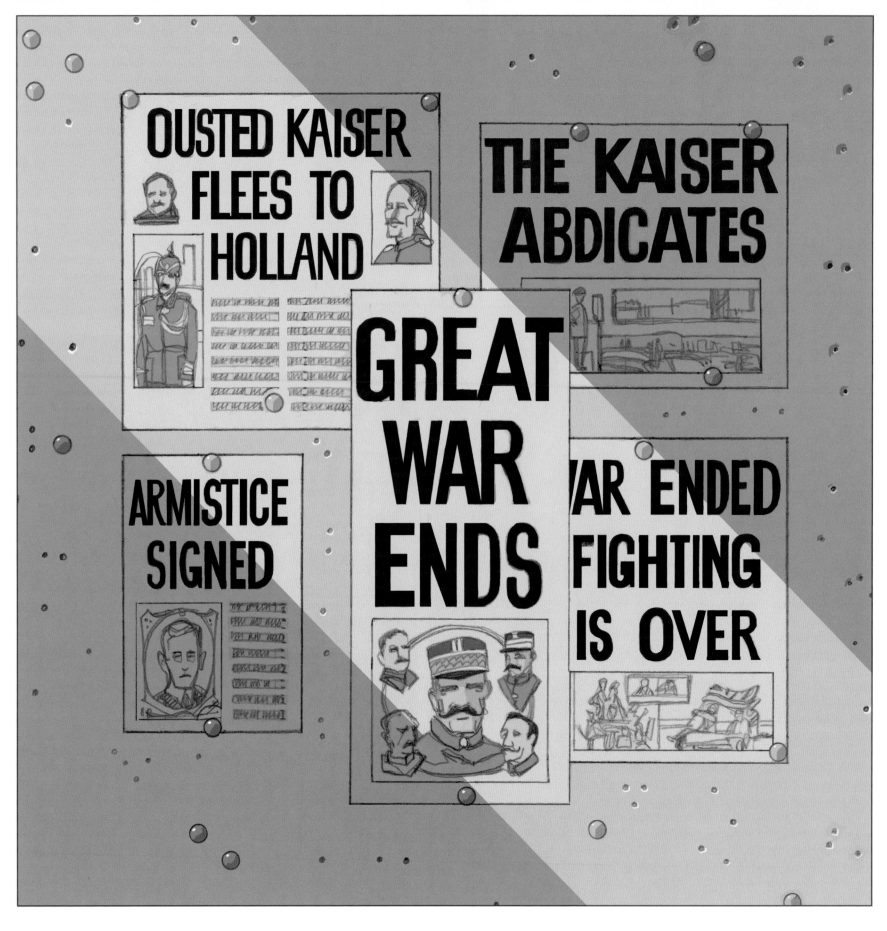

10 November 1918
Pasewalk Military Hospital, Germany

So it had all been in vain. In vain all the sacrifices … in vain the death of two millions. …
Hatred grew in me, hatred for those responsible for this deed. That night I resolved that,
if I recovered my sight, I would enter politics.

Corporal Adolf Hitler, 16th Bavarian Reserve

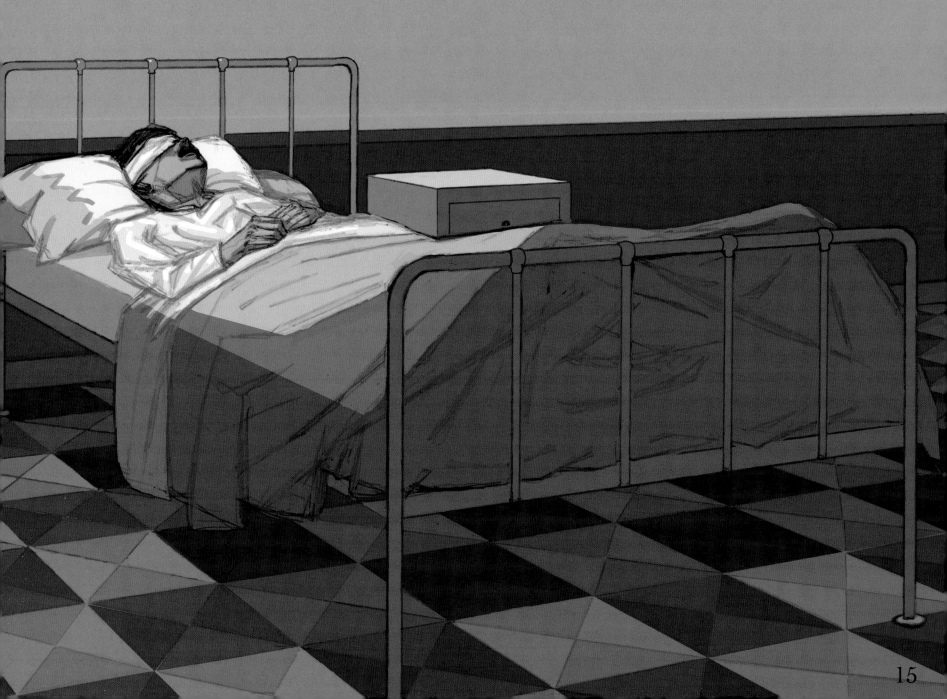

12 November 1918
Front Line, France

The day after the fighting ended I met hundreds of men who had been prisoners and broken out just before the Armistice. They were coming back into our lines, almost starving, and some of them had died of hunger and exhaustion on the way; but they came along splendidly, marching in little groups under the command of the oldest soldier in each, with their horrible black uniforms as clean and neat as hard trying could make them, marching along very steady and smart and taking no notice of anybody. I thought I had never seen the British soldier to better advantage.

Captain Charles Montague, Military Intelligence

November 1918

We are to return to Germany. The war is finished. That means the end of our flying. All of a sudden our strenuous activities are replaced by an empty nothing. Tomorrow there will no longer be a Jagdstaffel 35. On the map I write the date: 10.11.18. That was our last front line.

Leutnant (Lieutenant) Rudolf Stark, Leader, Jagdstaffel 35, Imperial German Air Service

November 1918

Back to the Rhine – back, back without a stop. The highways were crammed with moving men, endless lines of men, war equipment, guns, pack trains, lorries and horses. Through France and Belgium, the grey columns moved. Nobody knew what the future held but everybody's mind formed a belief of better days to come.

Unteroffizier (Sergeant) Frederick Meisel, 371st Infantry, Imperial German Army

14 November 1918
Near Amiens, northern France

Mama said now we could go home. But when we return there is no home, just a rubble of bricks and broken walls. The few trees are black skeletons. The wheatfields are mud. Most of our village has gone. Everything lies in ruin. 'We will rebuild,' says Mama. I start to cry because how can we, with Papa and my two uncles killed in the fighting? I want my old home back, and our horse, and our chickens, but Mama has brought a French flag on a stick and someone finds a ladder and Grandpère climbs up and plants it on top of a crumbling wall and then I feel better because it has been so long since we saw the Tricolour flying. Someone somewhere blows a trumpet and we turn to each other and smile.

The war is over!

Emile Fournier, 9

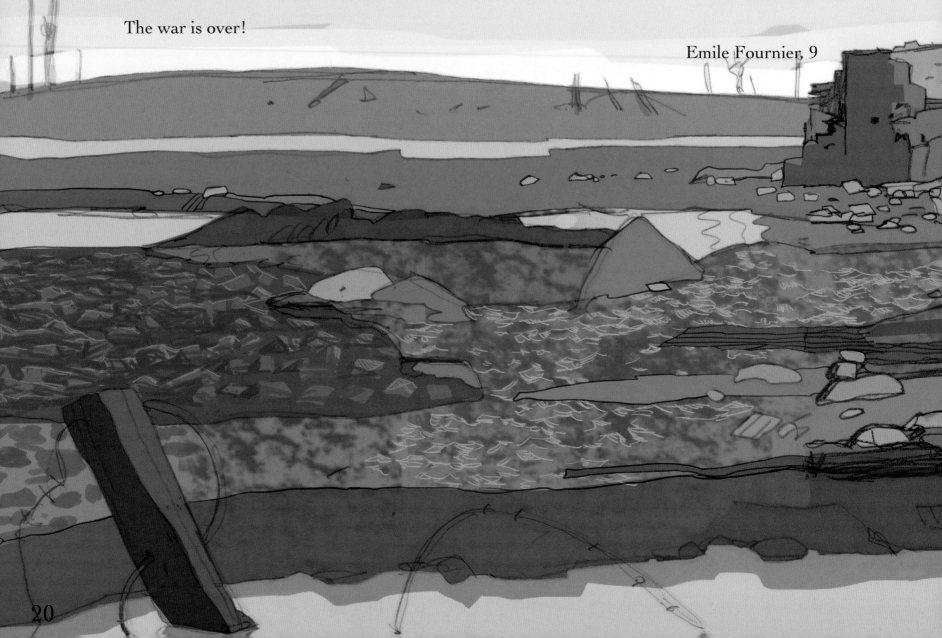

6 December 1918 – 10 am
Cologne, Germany

It was raining when we marched across the Hohenzollern Bridge over the Rhine and into Cologne, the first troops of the British occupying army. The streets were lined with thousands of people – all curious to see the enemy, I suppose – but they hardly made a sound. It was a queer feeling marching past those staring, silent crowds. There was no traffic. All you could hear was the tramp, tramp, tramp of our boots. Perhaps they cheered later, for the cavalry divisions, but probably not. They weren't in a cheering mood.

I must say we all looked very fit and fine in our uniforms compared to the locals, who mostly looked half-starved and very poorly turned out. The authorities have ordered all German men to raise their hats to our officers, which I dare say they won't like one bit.

When we came to the cathedral and lined up in our rows, an old bloke standing in the crowd caught my eye. Tears were running down his face, as if it had only just hit him that Germany had been defeated. He jerked his hand towards the Union Jack hanging limply in the rain and called out something that I didn't understand but I'm betting he won't be raising his hat.

Private Arthur Brown,
VI Corps, London Division,
British Army of the Rhine

Our time will come again.

Hermann Göring, German fighter pilot ace

May 1954
Paris

The way the Great War ended, with an armistice and with no fighting on German soil, had serious consequences. Most ordinary Germans did not accept that Germany was defeated and finished militarily; they did not regard 11 November as a day of surrender. This attitude affected everything that took place during the Peace Conference held in Versailles, near Paris, between January and June of 1919.

The Treaty of Versailles, as it was called, was much more than a formal declaration of the end of war. The peacemakers who drew it up – and it took them six months, not the four weeks they had promised – wanted to ensure that a world war would never happen again. They aimed to find new ways of protecting weaker countries and settling disputes. They dreamed of a peaceful world governed through a universal 'Parliament of Man', to be called the League of Nations. And they had to decide how much Germany should pay in reparation.

Once more I found myself at the centre of history as we again awaited the arrival of the German delegation, not to a train in a forest this time, but to the glorious Palace of Versailles. But to get here their train from Berlin had to pass through the ravaged and battle-scarred countryside of northern France. I heard that instructions were given to ensure their train travelled slowly and was halted several times: ample time for them to contemplate the devastating results of their warmongering.

Paul Mantoux, Chief Allied Interpreter

28 April 1919
Northern France

The first impression of the occupied areas seared my soul. Then came northern France!
It was a harrowing experience though we knew from pictures and descriptions what a
battlefield looks like.

Walter Simons, lawyer, German delegation

11 May 1919
Versailles, France

We are here to decide the issue of German guilt and,
ultimately, German reparation.

Georges Clemenceau, Prime Minister of France

In a war, who is innocent? There is guilt on all sides.

Count Ulrich von Brockdorff-Rantzau,
leader of German delegation

I speak for sixty thousand dead.

Billy Hughes, Prime Minister of Australia

How much longer must we repeat history before we
learn that revenge won't work?

Woodrow Wilson,
President of the United States

May 1919

There are more than 500 newspaper correspondents from all over the world here in Paris. We're being told almost nothing of the progress of the Peace Conference. I haven't been able to interview anyone and the official press announcements are vague. Months have gone by and what progress has been made? The Kaiser hasn't been hanged, the losers haven't yet paid a penny in reparations, the spoils of war haven't been divided. I can hear the rumbles of dissatisfaction from home, but all I can do is file copy criticising the 'dawdlers of Paris'.

War correspondent, *Manchester Guardian*

Do you know how many casualties we in the French Army suffered over the course of the war? Six million! We fought the Germans alone for more than two years while our Allies raised their armies, and the fighting was largely on French soil. It was French farms, French villages and French towns that were laid low, French lives that were lost. President Wilson should come and see the ruin with his own eyes; only then will he understand how big a debt the Allies owe to France.

French war veteran

At Versailles, the Big Four powers – Britain, France, Italy and the United States – debated among themselves for months how much Germany should pay, how much it could actually afford to pay, and how the reparation would be distributed. But in resolving this, and drawing new lines on the map of Europe, they made deals and compromises that signalled trouble for the future.

Paul Mantoux, Chief Allied Interpreter

I have promised Britain $120 billion.
    David Lloyd George, Prime Minister of Great Britain

The French demand $220 billion.
    Georges Clemenceau, Prime Minister of France

The United States recommends $22 billion.
    Woodrow Wilson, President of the United States

Germany can pay at most $10 billion.
    John Maynard Keynes, Chief British Treasury Advisor

THE PRICE GERMANY MUST PAY

ALSACE-LORRAINE GOES TO FRANCE

POLAND GAINS TERRITORY

COLONIES TO BE RENOUNCED

Count Ulrich von Brockdorff-Rantzau

INDEMNITY - £5,000,000,000 ON ACCOUNT REMAINDER TO BE FIXED

The Allies must recognise that it is impossible to burden a country with debts and at the same time deprive it of the means of paying them.

Max Warburg, banker, German delegation

"Let's see you collect it."

28 June 1919
Palace of Versailles

From the forts in Paris and the hills around Versailles comes the tremendous boom of cannons, and suddenly the fountains in the park, which were turned off at the beginning of the war, are gushing heavenward. 'The Treaty has been signed!' my sister says excitedly.

We look across to the terrace and see Mr Clemenceau, Mr Lloyd George and President Wilson coming out to see the fountains. The crowd around us surges forward. They push past the police cordons and troops, and cheer and wave flags, and we are swept along with them. The three men wander onto the grass, looking very pleased with themselves, and then a bit worried as people begin grasping their hands and pounding their backs. President Wilson is nearly pushed into a fountain!

My sister squeezes my hand. 'Imagine, Claudine, no more wars!'

—Claudine Lafleur, 16

28 June 1919
Berlin

Vengeance, people of Germany! Today the shameful treaty has been signed in the Hall of Mirrors at Versailles. Today, German honour is there interred. Do not forget it! By ceaseless labour and without flagging the German people will reconquer the place among the nations which is their due. Then will come revenge for the ignominy of 1919!

Front page editorial, *Deutsche Zeitung*

You may strip Germany of her colonies, reduce her armaments to a mere police force and her navy to that of a fifth-rate power; all the same, in the end, if she feels that she has been unjustly treated in the peace of 1919, she will find means of exacting retribution from her conquerors.
David Lloyd George, Prime Minister of Great Britain

At Versailles, at the drawing up of the Treaty, I warned that only permanent Allied occupation of the Rhineland would protect France from future German aggression. I was not heeded: the occupation would last a mere fifteen years. As the Treaty was being signed I prophesied: 'This is not a peace. It is an armistice for twenty years.'

Ferdinand Foch, Marshal of France and Supreme Allied Commander

1 October 1939
Warsaw, Poland

Exactly twenty years and sixty-four days after the Treaty was
signed Germany invaded Poland, and a month later German troops
marched in and occupied Warsaw. Britain and France declared war
on Germany, and the world was once again at war.

Page 2

An **armistice** is a cessation of hostilities as a prelude to peace negotiations.

The **Austro-Hungarian Empire** was a union of the kingdoms of Austria and Hungary. Created in 1867 and ruled by the House of Habsburg, it was one of the world's great powers before it surrendered in 1918 and split into Austria, Hungary, Yugoslavia and Czechoslovakia.

The **Balkans** refers to the countries that lie between Russia, Austria-Hungary and Turkey, such as Bosnia and Serbia.

Nicholas II (1868–1918), a first cousin of King George V of England, was the last of the Romanov tsars (emperors) of Russia. He and his family were murdered by **Bolsheviks** in 1918. The **Bolsheviks** were members of the Russian Democratic Party, led by Lenin, who seized control of the government in 1917.

The **Western Front** – the series of trenches that formed a boundary between the German army and the Allied forces – was the main theatre of war. The main **Allied powers** were Britain and its Empire (including Australia), France, Russia and the United States.

The **East African campaign** began in August 1914 in German East Africa (the region around the African Great Lakes, encompassing Burundi, Rwanda and Tanganyika), and spread to Mozambique, Northern Rhodesia, British East Africa, Uganda and the Belgian Congo. It ended on 25 November 1918, the day after news of the Armistice finally reached troops fighting in the region.

 Paul Joseph Mantoux (1877–1956) was Professor of Modern French History at the University of London when he was recruited in 1914 to act as interpreter for the general staff of a British army division in Flanders. He rose to become Chief Allied Interpreter at the 1919 Paris Peace Conference. His words here are imagined.

Page 4

 Ferdinand Jean Marie Foch (1851–1929), a French general and Marshal of France, was the Supreme Allied Commander during the final year of the First World War.

Page 5

 In 1916, aged 18, **Erich Maria Remarque** was drafted into the German army and was badly wounded in the fighting. Ten years after the war ended, he published *Im Westen nichts Neues*, translated into English a year later as *All Quiet on the Western Front*, a novel about the experiences of ordinary German soldiers during the war. It quickly became an international bestseller. This quotation is from the final pages of the novel.

Pages 6–7

 The Royal Navy's primary task throughout the First World War was the **blockade** of Germany, restricting the importation of food and materials to the enemy and starving the German people into submission. An estimated 424,000 German civilians died from starvation and disease. This account is based on information from *The Home Fronts: Britain, France and Germany, 1914–1918*, by John Williams (Constable, 1972).

Pages 8–9

 Kaiser Wilhelm II (1859–1941), a grandson of Queen Victoria and first cousin to King George V of England, was the last **kaiser** (emperor) of Germany. He was forced to abdicate on 9 November 1918, and spent the rest of his life in exile in The Netherlands.

Matthias Erzberger (1875–1921) was Vice-Chancellor and Finance Minister in the first government of the new German Republic. He signed the Armistice agreement for Germany at Compiègne and directed all negotiations with the Allies at Versailles. In 1921 he was assassinated in Berlin by right-wing terrorists.

Under the terms of the Armistice, Germany lost 5,000 artillery pieces, 30,000 machine-guns, 3,000 mine-launchers, 2,000 aircraft, 5,000 locomotives, 150,000 railway wagons, 5,000 trucks and its entire submarine fleet. The majority of the surface naval fleet was surrendered; the remainder was disbanded.

Pages 10–11

Harry S. Truman (1884–1972) became the 33rd President of the United States (1945–53). During the First World War he served as a field artillery officer, commanding Battery D of the 129th Field Artillery in France. The words quoted are taken from the Truman

(continued)

Papers held in the Harry S. Truman Library and Museum. The French village named is Hermeville-en-Woëvre, in the district of Verdun.

Thomas Russell Gowenlock's memories of the Armistice are taken from his book, co-written with Guy Murchie, *Soldiers of Darkness* (Doubleday, 1937).

Walter C. Belford's words are taken from his book *Legs-eleven: being the story of the 11th Battalion (A.I.F.) in the Great War of 1914–1918* (Imperial Printing Co.,1940).

Malcolm Cowley (1898–1989) was one of the many young Americans living in Paris at the outbreak of the First World War who volunteered to drive ambulances. He also reported from the Western Front for the *Pittsburgh Gazette*. His words are taken from his memoir *Exile's Return* (Viking Press, 1934).

Edward C. Allfree's words are quoted in *1918: A Very British Victory*, by Peter Hart (Weidenfeld & Nicolson, 2008). Allfree's diary is held by the Imperial War Museum, London.

Page 15

While serving in the Bavarian Reserve Infantry, Regiment 16, in October 1918 **Adolf Hitler** (1889–1945) was partially blinded in a mustard-gas attack near Ypres. He was sent to the Pasewalk Military Hospital where news of the Armistice reached him on 10 November as he was convalescing. The German capitulation sent him into a deep depression. The quotation is from his autobiography and political manifesto *Mein Kampf*, or *My Struggle* (1925; first English publication 1933).

Pages 16–17

Charles Edward Montague (1867–1928) was an English journalist and author who, despite his age (47), wife and seven children, enlisted in the British Army in 1914 after dyeing his grey hair black. He became a captain of Intelligence in 1915 and worked as an army censor, censoring articles written by the five authorised English journalists on the Western Front. He also took distinguished visitors on tours of the front line trenches. The words quoted come from a letter he wrote on 18 November 1918 to Francis Dodd (1874–1949), an official war artist.

Pages 18–19

Rudolf Stark (1897–1982) was a German flying ace. His squadron Jagdstaffel 35 was a Royal Bavarian fighting squadron of the air service of the Imperial German Army during the First World War. The quotation comes from his best-selling memoir, *Wings of War: A German Airman's Diary of the Last Year of the Great War*, translated by Claud W. Sykes (Military Books, 1973).

The words of **Frederick Meisel** are quoted in *The Road Home: The Aftermath of the Great War Told by the Men and Women Who Survived It*, by Max Arthur (Hachette, 2014).

Pages 20–21

Amiens in northern France was important to the Allies as a major rail hub through which supplies were moved to the front line. The Battle of Amiens in August 1918 was an Allied victory. It helped bring an end to the war, but it cost over 21,000 Allied casualties and left the countryside totally devastated.

Pages 22–23

The British army of occupation remained in Germany for ten years. This first **British Army of the Rhine** (BAOR) was based in the Rhineland around Cologne, and included army, cavalry and tank corps, plus staff and supporting ancillary services. In 1920 the BAOR comprised approximately 13,300 troops.

Pages 24–25

Hermann Wilhelm Göring (1893–1946) helped Hitler take power in 1933, founded the Gestapo, or secret political police, and in 1935 was appointed commander of the German air force. Hitler named him his successor in 1939, making him the second most powerful man in Germany.

The peacemakers who drew up the Treaty of Versailles had to decide on the amount of **reparation**: the money Germany had to pay for damage done during the war. Reparations would go primarily to France, the country most affected by the war, and towards costs in other countries, including Belgium. The amount was calculated to be 132 billion gold marks, or US$33 billion, on top of the initial £5 billion (US$22 billion) payment demanded by the Treaty. Germany stopped paying the reparations in 1933 after the Nazi Party took power.

The League of Nations, set up under the provisions of the Treaty of Versailles, was the first international organisation formed to maintain international peace and was the forerunner of today's United Nations.

Pages 26–27
Walter Simons (1861–1937), a German lawyer and colleague of Foreign Minister Ulrich von Brockdorff-Rantzau, was appointed Under-Secretary and accompanied the German delegation to Versailles for the Peace Conference in 1919. He opposed signing the Treaty and resigned his post. The words quoted are from a letter to his wife.

On their arrival in Paris in early May, members of the German delegation were presented with their copies of the Treaty of Versailles, which had been drawn up in the preceding months by their victorious enemies. They were aghast when they read the demands made by the Allies.

Pages 28–29

Georges Clemenceau (1841–1929) was a statesman and journalist who served as Prime Minister of France (1917–1920) and was the senior French representative at Versailles.

Count Ulrich von Brockdorff-Rantzau (1869–1928), a career diplomat, was the leader of the German delegation to the Paris Peace Conference. He objected to the terms demanded by the Allies and refused to sign the Treaty. (It was signed instead by Hermann Müller, the German Prime Minister.)

William (Billy) Hughes (1862–1952) was Australia's seventh prime minister (1915–1923) at a time when the population was five million. At Paris, when the American President Wilson, whose country had only entered the war a year before its end, questioned Hughes's authority to intervene in world affairs, Hughes responded: 'I speak for sixty thousand dead. For how many do you speak?'

Thomas Woodrow Wilson (1856–1924) was the 28th President of the United States, serving from 1913 to 1921. The first American president to visit Europe while in office, at the Paris Peace Conference he was the driving force behind the establishment of the League of Nations.

Pages 32–33
French Prime Minister Clemenceau wanted to totally crush Germany. 'We must finish the job, for the dead and those yet to be born,' he said. Most of France agreed with him.

John Maynard Keynes (1883–1946), a brilliant economist, acted as the British Treasury's chief representative at the Paris Peace Conference. He criticised the massive reparations demanded of Germany, rightly predicting that it would foster a desire for revenge, and argued that Germany did not have the capacity to pay the entire cost of the war.

Page 35
Max Moritz Warburg (1867–1946) was a German–Jewish banker from a wealthy Hamburg banking family. Pre-war, he was an adviser to Kaiser Wilhelm, and during the war to German politicians, diplomats and the military. In 1919 he was an economic specialist with the German delegation to Versailles. In 1938, when the Nazis forced the closure of the Warburg Bank, he emigrated to the USA.

The cartoon 'Let's see you collect it' was published in *New York World* in 1921. The New York City-based daily (1860–1931) was known for its numerous outstanding reporters, editors and cartoonists and was closely associated with Joseph Pulitzer who purchased the paper in 1883.

Pages 38–39
Deutsche Zeitung (literally, 'German newspaper') was a Berlin-based national newspaper.

Pages 42–43
Hitler claimed that his invasion of Poland was a defensive action, but Britain and France, both allies of Poland, thought otherwise. On 3 September 1939 they declared war on Germany. Poland remained under German occupation until January 1945.

Page 44

The **Holocaust** was the mass murder of millions of people in Europe by Nazi Germany during the Second World War. At least six million of them were Jews, including over one million children. The Nazis built a number of concentration or extermination camps, such as Auschwitz, for the sole purpose of killing large numbers of people quickly and efficiently.

For Jane – R.S.

For Vokili, Mieke and Piper – D. K.

This project has been assisted by the May Gibbs Children's Literature
Trust through its Creative Time Residential Fellowship program

MAY GIBBS
Children's Literature Trust

The characters portrayed in this book are both fictitious and real. Where
applicable, the Notes at the back of the book provide biographical details
of those who recorded their experiences and memories of this period.

Working Title Press
An imprint of HarperCollins*Children'sBooks*, Australia

First published in Australia in 2018
by HarperCollins*Publishers* Australia Pty Limited
ABN 36 009 913 517
harpercollins.com.au

HarperCollins*Publishers*
Level 13, 201 Elizabeth Street, Sydney NSW 2000, Australia
Unit D1, 63 Apollo Drive, Rosedale, Auckland 0632, New Zealand

A catalogue record for this book is available from the National Library of Australia

ISBN: 978 1 921504 91 4

Designed and set in Cochin by Greg Holfeld, Panic Productions
The illustrations in this book were done in graphite pencil and coloured in Photoshop
Colour reproduction by Graphic Print Group, South Australia
Printed and bound in China by RR Donnelley on 128gsm Matt Art

5 4 3 2 1   18 19 20 21

EUROPE
1925

IRISH FREE STATE

UNITED KINGDOM

Paris○

FRANCE

PORTUGAL

SPAIN